ALL IN ONE RIVER

FALLS DAM TO PAMLICO SOUND—
INTERVIEWING THE NEUSE RIVER

Ben Casey

CHAPEL HILL
PRESS, INC.

WITH GRATITUDE TO THE FOLLOWING

Edwina Woodbury
Stephanie Greene
Katie Severa
Misty Thebeau

THE CHAPEL HILL PRESS—CHAPEL HILL, NORTH CAROLINA

Natalie Baggett & Rebecca Book

THE NEUSE RIVER FOUNDATION—NEW BERN, NORTH CAROLINA

John Hinners

MERRITT, NORTH CAROLINA

Bob Andrews and Earl Evens

ORIENTAL, NORTH CAROLINA

Gene Wooster

MOBILE EAST MARINE—PAMLICO COUNTY, NORTH CAROLINA

Ken & Dave Eason

KEN'S GRILL—LA GRANGE, NORTH CAROLINA

Copyright © 2003 Benjamin Earl Casey

All Rights Reserved. No part of this book may be used, reproduced or transmitted in any form or by any means, electronic or mechanical, including photocopy, recording or any information storage or retrieval system, without the express written permission of the publisher, except where permitted by law.

ISBN Number 1-880849-51-8
Manufactured in the United States of America
Library of Congress 2002112268
Second Edition
2004

FOR EMMY

With special thanks to

Dave Mauney

Ken Brandon

Richard de Charms

Marny Muir

and

The Neusiok Indians

The River Trip...

A Personal Perspective

Just as a river can transform its flow from a small rocky streambed into a major water highway serving ocean-going vessels, first impressions can float from a trickle to a running current of emotions and reactions.

I remember that as a young child I was so impressed growing up in and around New Bern to learn that the Neuse River Bridge was a mile long, the river was a mile wide.

As a student, I learned the Eno and Flat Rivers merged in Durham County to form the Neuse. To quench the thirst of the constantly burgeoning Raleigh-Durham area, Falls Dam was erected near Wake Forest to create the massive Falls Lake, hiding the former streambed of the river under thousands of acres of the new reservoir.

Though the Neuse visits several towns of major interest on its southeastward journey to the Pamlico Sound—Raleigh, Clayton, Wilson's Mills, Smithfield, Brogden, Seven Springs, Kinston, Sand Hill, Maple Cypress, Spring Garden, New Bern, James City and Oriental—there is always the feeling when one is on the Neuse that civilization is a universe away. This is even the case where outer runway markers have been planted in the river for the world's most advanced fighter jets at Seymour Johnson Air Force Base in Wayne County.

On the river, one learns that the drama unfolding when a heron lifts off in flight will grab the senses with as much passion as watching Top Gun lift off a carrier's deck.

Speaking of flight, on this river I saw my first bald eagle.

I am neither historian nor scientist. This book is not about Neuse River history or the science of river eco-systems. This is an effort to share the beauty of the river and emotional reactions to that beauty.

It is difficult for the printed page to relate the drama of a shad swimming so near that it bumps into the side of the canoe. What about the intensity of feelings when dolphins half as long as your skiff swim beneath your bow? How can any photograph really depict the foliage—from river birch to willow oaks, from pine trees to cypress knees?

What about the sounds?

Can the printed page reveal the melody carried by a warbler perched on a cypress knee serenading two men in a canoe?

How can a reader feel the oxymoronic blend of tranquility and excitement, basted with anxiety, as those in a canoe learn of upcoming whitewater by hearing first the sound of the water rushing over and between rock formations?

Perhaps the reader can draw upon the wisdom of Albert Einstein, who observed that imagination is more valuable than acquired knowledge.

This endeavor was not a river trip adventure. It was a mission to see and record on film and paper all the dynamics of the contrasts that lie between Falls Dam and Pamlico Sound on every inch of this water highway.

The Neuse River should never have been a dumping ground for man's waste. It is more than a faucet for man's thirst or a theme park for water sports.

I want this book to reveal to the people of North Carolina, and elsewhere, an opportunity for them to know what a treasure this river is …a treasure of infinite value.

The River... A Grand and Noble Gift

Great people have had great things to say about the terrain that is home.

Washington Irving is quoted as saying, "I thank God I was born on the banks of the Hudson! I think it an invaluable advantage to be born and brought up in the neighborhood of some grand and noble object in nature: a river, a lake, or a mountain. We make a friendship with it; we in a manner ally ourselves with it for life."

More recently,. Frances Mauney, ninety-two years young, who grew up on the banks of the Upper Neuse River near Clayton, North Carolina, said, "The character of the land where a man grows up helps determine the character of the man."

What is the character of the Neuse River, two million years old, whose banks were first settled by Native Americans 14,000 years ago? How differently did those early settlers, the Tuscaroras, Coree, Neusiok and Secotan tribes, interact with the river from the one and one-half million people who live in this watershed today?

Today's population mixes recreational use of the river with using the river as a reservoir for drinking water or for discharging wastewater.

From its headwaters, the Neuse flows downstream more than two hundred miles to the Pamlico Sound, part of the Albemarle-Pamlico estuarine system, the second largest estuarine system in the United States. The mouth of the Neuse at its junction with the Pamlico Sound is the widest mouth of any river in the continental United States.

Volumes can be written detailing demographic data about the Neuse and its river basin. While satisfying trivia buffs, would this information really translate what one feels by actually being on the river?

Rather than list such facts and figures, these photographs and essays will attempt to convey the feelings characterized by Washington Irving and Frances Mauney, feelings that evolve and grow from each excursion amongst the ripples and waves.

I thank God I was born on the banks of the Neuse. Growing up and living on, or near, this river has led me to the feelings expressed by Laura Hutchinson, chaplain of my Alma Mater, Atlantic Christian College in Wilson, North Carolina.

Hutchinson says, "As a human being and a Christian, I feel that I have been given the supreme responsibility to take care of this

world that God created and then entrusted to humanity. Our earth and everything on it is a gift, not something owed to us, and thus, we must care for it properly."

She says that with the great power we have acquired in having dominion over our environment, there comes great responsibility. She adds, "Though we have been given free will and absolute ownership over the earth, we absolutely have no right to destroy it. What we have is a duty to preserve it, to protect it, and to take care of it as if the earth were something of infinite value that its owner has asked us to keep for just a while."

The one and a half million people who live in this river basin have been given this gift, to be brought up in the neighborhood of this grand and noble object in nature, the Neuse River.

It is my hope that this body of work will encourage more to make a friendship with the river and in a manner, ally one's self with it for life. Such a relationship will lead one to embrace the river as a gift of infinite value.

"Water is the element of feeling. I become one with all things when I blend water and my sense of touch. No more alone. Everything is accomplished through the senses," said American painter Walter Anderson to his wife after a night swim in the Ohio River.

As a photographer, I feel I lack the command of language enjoyed by artists, philosophers, and poets. They can perhaps better relate sensitivity to the elements of nature that cultivate man's feelings. I can sense a great reaction from within to a scene on the Neuse through my camera lens, but the printed photograph, no matter how striking, cannot match the feeling of being by, or on, the water.

Viewing a photograph of morning mist floating above the current in the Neuse while the rising sun creeps through to highlight the branches of a single tree, can heighten our appreciation for what the river offers, but it is still only a substitute for actually being there.

Water is more than the element of feeling. Water is the genesis of feeling.

I once owned a motorcycle.

Even though reading Robert Pirsig's *Zen and the Art of Motorcycle Maintenance* led me to become somewhat of a biker after my fourteenth midlife crisis, Pirsig would have been critical of my attitude about riding.

A major theme throughout his book is the clash between the classical and the romantic. Pirsig said that some people focused too much on the classical in life, maintaining a motorcycle, while others were too carefree as romantics, wanting to enjoy only the thrill of the ride.

He contended that those with a classical orientation were happier adjusting the valves than actually riding. On the other hand, the romantic was so enamored with the thrill of riding, he might not know the motorcycle engine had valves.

Pirsig believed that a proper and balanced approach to all of life's mysteries was a blend of the classical and the romantic.

Though I recognize the value of, and appreciate the need for, the classical, I am an unashamed romantic.

I launched this discourse because I felt the need to rationalize the fact that I could appreciate and marvel at the flowers that are all in one river basin, but couldn't, for the life of me, identify them by either their scientific or common names.

Yes, an appreciation for flora and fauna would be enhanced with more classical knowledge, but that doesn't diminish my capacity to be in awe of the natural beauty of blooms hanging on the ends of vines wrapped around trees and stumps all along the river shore.

I could safely identify the water lilies along the edge of cypress swamps just west of New Bern, but not so for so many other petals and stems.

My inability to be well versed in botany is in no way an indication of my inability to marvel at the beauty of the varied plant life along the Neuse

I am thankful for classical botanists. Their work helps us know more about the life of the river and how to protect it.

O ne doesn't necessarily have to know the name of a bird to see, or hear, its contribution to the beauty of being outdoors.

With my brain falling more to the right than to the left, so many birds fall into the category known as "lgb"—little gray bird.

Just about everyone can recognize the sight and sound of the river's town crier, the kingfisher. He's joined by every bird imaginable common to Eastern North Carolina, from tiny humming birds to the great blue heron, from pelicans to Canada geese, from Cardinals to mallards, from ospreys to snowy egrets, from crows to seagulls.

When I was fifty-four, I saw my first bald eagle on this river just west of the power plant at Goldsboro. Too far away for a photograph good enough for publication, it was close enough to make me feel as though I was looking at a stunning scene in a wildlife magazine.

The birds, bees, and their trees—just more reasons to appreciate this grand and noble river.

Birds

Fallen leaves, transporting drops of water that become prisms reflecting rainbows of sunlight, are perhaps the most beautiful and natural things floating down the river.

Humongous logs and branches floated by past hurricanes are still snagged in the tops of trees overhanging the river and up under the bottom of the roadbeds of bridges. Not necessarily adding much to the scenery along the river, such flotsam is at least a part of the natural consequence of the forces of nature.

Then there's all that plastic left behind by man floated by those very same forces of nature. Some of it is easy to figure out. It's understandable that the flood of Hurricane Floyd would transport a highway barricade down the river.

But how did a basketball and a pickle jar wind up floating on a big black piece of foam rubber?

Sadly, we all know how an empty Gatorade bottle came to float by.

"Don't burn any bridges."

"Cross that bridge when you come to it."

Bridges are often used by philosophers to impart wisdom, but a fascination with bridges goes beyond those engineering marvels allowing man to ford streams.

Novels, movies, and songs allude to the mystical and mysterious. What did Billie Joe McAlister toss off that bridge? How did those prisoners of war reach for that fortitude it took to build The Bridge over the River Kwai? And wasn't a bridge a pivotal point for Jimmy Stewart in "It's A Wonderful Life?"

Bridges over the Neuse River may not have yet been immortalized by Hollywood. That's not to say they don't play a romantic part in the lives of residents of Eastern North Carolina, or citizens of the world for that matter, crossing over the I-95 Bridge in Johnston County. More people from more far-reaching places cross the Neuse on Interstate 95, but those local folks who cross over the almost antique two-lane span on Maple Cypress Road near the Craven-Lenoir County line have a closer connection with the river.

For locals, bridges are more than a way to cross. They represent a community of social landmarks. People gather at bridges to fish, to picnic, and to simply while away time.

Consequently, many bridges have names that honor local heroes. Who was Sam Casey? Why was the NC581 bridge in Wayne county named after him?

Then there's the gargantuan complex of twisting concrete ribbons that towers sixty-five feet above the Neuse at New Bern. Granted, it's convenient not to have to wait for the old draw-bridge to open for a passing tugboat or a tall masted sailboat. Commuters on their way to work no longer have to lament being held up by people passing in pleasure boats too tall to pass under the bridge. Gone are the excuses one could offer for being late for appointments or late coming home because they were caught by the drawbridge. All of that may be history, but the old drawbridge did have character.

On NC Highway 306 from Minnesott to Cherry Branch, the ferry is the bridge offering a real connection with the river. There, two ferry boats, one aptly named "Neuse," both longer than all the river crossings except New Bern, can transport forty cars apiece across that three-mile expanse of choppy waves in less than twenty minutes.

For those who are in constant yearning to feel the river, twenty minutes is far too short a time to share and savor the crossing with laughing gulls, pelicans, and cormorants. The ferry offers a grand and unique opportunity for its passengers to share the river in fellowship with one another.

Looking back at my journey from Falls Dam to the Pamlico Sound, passing under so many bridges and railroad trestles, I felt sorry for the souls zipping across overhead not able to reach out and touch water.

Those bridging the river at the Minnesott-Cherry Branch ferry crossing understand how I could reach that conclusion.

For fun, imagine a ferry crossing for I-95 across the Neuse.

So, one can have a love affair with bridges of great character as well a romance with crossing on the water.

Fascinated with the river and loving being on it as much as I do, a dream come true for me was the opportunity to work on a ferry. In so many ways, it was absolutely the best job in the world.

"Isn't that about the most boring job in the world?"

"What's somebody with your education doing parking cars on a ferry boat?"

I heard these queries and more.

After a few months, I quit to take a job with a newspaper in an effort to further my wannabe career in writing. I had been disappointed to be assigned to work at the Pamlico River Ferry, somewhat of a drive from my home, instead of the Neuse River Ferry which I can see in the distance from my front yard.

I often regret quitting and I miss the work I did which afforded me the opportunity to both help and interact with ferry passengers. Much to the credit of administrators of the Ferry Division, a great deal of emphasis is placed on passenger safety as well as service.

While ferry employees work diligently to provide safe passage and comfort for the passengers, I always felt my work went way beyond guiding a car to a parking space on the boat. Riding a boat across a river is not just a means to get from one side of the river to the other. It's an experience. I was eager for the passengers to share my enthusiasm for this experience.

When ferries transport tourists, it's easy to feel the excitement glowing in the eyes of little children, especially first time riders. For the everyday commuters, the ferry offers therapeutic downtime from the stress of work and travel. The ferry is a highway painted with sights and sounds from nature, as opposed to a highway of asphalt painted with billboards and reminders of a more frantic pace.

When Hurricane Floyd wreaked havoc on Eastern North Carolina bridges, the Ferry Division and ferry workers responded with uncommon valor in transporting the passengers that normally would have taken the bridge at Little Washington to cross the Pamlico River.

Ferries have been bridges for the Neuse River since settlers began to populate this river basin in the 18th century. Like bridges, they have often been focal points for communities.

A bridge across a body of water connects one side of that body of water with the other. A ferry crossing a body of water connects its riders with the water.

The ferry, like a chair along the riverbank, offers an opportunity for one to ponder.

How boring for someone to think riding a ferry could be boring.

The Ferry

I once had a conversation with Thomas Kenworthy of Oriental about how computers and the digital age had helped create a society that was only satisfied by instant gratification. The dialogue was focused on how citizens in the age of technology are always in a hurry.

Thomas observed, "Nobody takes time any more to ponder. People sometimes just need to sit and ponder things."

Fortunately, in my trip down the river from Falls Dam to Pamlico Sound, I discovered that the river, at least, was apparently inspiring people to sit and ponder things.

What better place than a riverbank to sit and dream, to think of things that never were and ask, "Why not?"

There is a kind of spiritual magnetism about a river—upriver along the rocky streambed, mid-river marked by sandbars and willow oaks, or the wide- open expanse of downriver— that entices people to sit and ponder things.

All along the river, there are chairs poised for pondering which might really be there for fishing. Washing a fishing hook in the river under the pretense of fishing is the greatest way to ponder the puzzles of life. Other chairs are there purely for the sake of pondering.

There are designer-made swings for the romantic couple, and folding chairs of various description. The grandest of all was the plastic relic of a chair whose missing back legs had been replaced by a piece of a log.

Anyone who would go to such lengths to keep a remnant of a plastic chair serviceable for pondering has to be someone who takes pondering by the river very seriously.

A soul is vastly enriched when pondering by the river, serenaded by warblers, entertained by kingfishers, inspired by eagles, observed by hawks, laughed at by black-faced gulls, squawked at by herons, and simply intrigued by all the visual and audible imagery flowing in, on, and by, the current.

Upriver, one ponders life while watching the moving currents. Downriver, one ponders life while watching the ebb and flow of the tide.

The river encourages pondering.

Fishing

It has been said, "Give a man a fish and you feed him one meal, teach a man to fish and you feed him for a lifetime."

It has also been theorized that crime and juvenile delinquency would be vastly diminished if more fathers would simply take little boys fishing. And I still recall the day my little girl caught her very first fish, a croaker, from a pier on the Neuse River.

The Neuse River offers an abundant harvest. Though two hundred miles of the river is habitat for fresh-water fish, the last forty miles of brackish water are often teeming with blue crabs, shrimp and fish common to salt water.

I didn't take this journey down the Neuse to catalogue all the fish species in this one river. That would be an overwhelming task. But what an experience it was to talk to Richard Wiggins and George Anderson, fishing for crappie in a tiny jon boat near Vanceboro, and then downstream in the same river photograph eighty-foot steel-hulled trawlers harvesting seafood by the ton.

There was that morning in Wayne County when I encountered a father and son duo with a cooler full of catfish the size of which would have just been another fish tale if I hadn't seen them myself. At the same time in Pamlico County, coolers were being loaded with catches of speckled trout.

Most remarkably, there was that morning in Wake County when what appeared to be a shad kept swimming right up to the canoe, close enough so I could have reached out and grabbed it. It did swim fast enough that it was hard to focus the camera on him, but at least one shot was good enough to prove this was not just another yarn spun by a would-be fisherman.

Another trial and error method with the camera came every time I tried to snare bottle-nosed dolphins in my lens in the lower Neuse. Watching a six-foot dolphin swim right beneath the bow of my Carolina skiff was quite a contrast to having a ten-inch shad bump into the canoe way upriver.

Then there was that hot afternoon in Lenoir County. Anglers fishing in tournaments passed my canoe at breakneck speeds. I wondered just how fast a bass could swim that such a powerful engine was needed to catch up with them.

While technology has transformed commercial fishing as an industry, those casting nets from small boats along the rivershore for flounder or trout are doing exactly the same thing Peter was doing in biblical times. About the only thing different is an engine on the boat and perhaps a plastic, dime-store chair for a little more comfort.

Some men fish for fun.
Some men fish for a meal.

Some men fish for a lifetime earning a living for their families while providing food for many.

Old-timers say fishing is not as good as it used to be.

Those whose souls are enriched by water usually try to live as close to the water as possible. Real estate agents use nomenclatures like Water View, Water Access or Waterfront to appeal to those for whom water generates great feelings.

Though my soul is enriched in a river home, I know there is not room for everyone to have this good fortune. I also know that an abode by the water can put the water at great risk.

Houses protect us from the elements. That should not come at the expense of protecting the river.

I let God nourish my yard. If God wants it to be green from rain or brown from lack of rain, I don't interfere. Not interfering with nature, I create no unnatural run-off.

There is greater value in living by the water than simply living in a fancy abode.

Some build classic structures that become historic landmarks. Some apparently use whatever floats up in recent floods to construct a riverside abode ... whatever works for the soul.

Abodes

Boats

Because the Neuse River is so wide, so narrow, so shallow, and so deep, the widest possible spectrum of vessels can ply at least some part of the river. Everything, from one-horse kayaks to sailing vessels that circumnavigate the globe, has floated on this river.

Canoes, jon boats, and high speed bass boats share the upper river. In the lower river, they are joined by ocean-going tugs and yachts, sport fishing boats, and commercial fishing vessels.

Captains on sailboats and sport fishing boats often choose whimsical boat names— *New Song*, *Reel Perspective*, or *Odyssey*, to name a few. On the other hand, workboats and fishing vessels are usually named for wives, girlfriends, or fathers—*Miss Alice*, *Miss Tammy*, or *Capt. Garland*.

Perhaps the most appropriate name of all adorns the transom of a commercial crab boat in Pamlico County. Some guy had it right when he named his boat— *The Boat*.

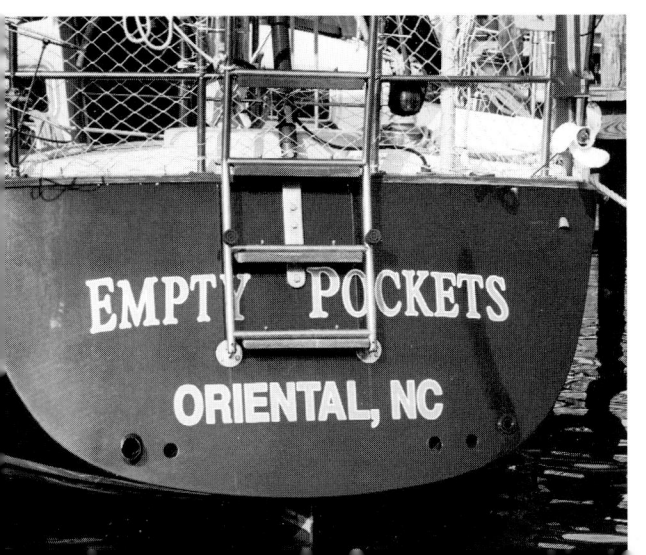

Cliffs

The folks of Whitehall on the banks of the Neuse River just southeast of Goldsboro were down for a while, but not out. The Yankees came in 1862 and burned the town. The citizens rose from the ashes to rebuild and to capitalize on local natural resources: seven springs allegedly producing mineral waters to cure every malady; the Neuse River; and that unbelievable ten story high, six hundred yard long bank on the river known as the Cliffs of the Neuse. The town was aptly renamed Seven Springs.

Tourists visiting this new resort in the late 19th century were treated to moonlight ferry rides upriver to the Cliffs for twenty-five cents.

I, most likely just like those tourists, did not really know what geological wonder I was witness to. When I first saw the Cliffs rising high from the riverbed, I immediately assumed that through the eons of time, the river had carved out this high bank, just as the Colorado River carved out the Grand Canyon.

But where was the wall on the other side of the Neuse? Across the river from the Cliffs, the terrain was as flat as the Coastal Plain. It didn't dawn on me at the time that if the river carves out a canyon, one would expect the canyon to have walls, or cliffs, to rise up from both sides of the river.

Not until I read a feature story by Marshall Ellis did I understand that it was some bumping and grinding of the earth's crust 130 million years ago that created the Cliffs in much the same fashion that the Appalachian Mountains were created. During that period, North Carolina's Coastal Plain was part of an ocean. Consequently, it is natural that the Cliffs are made up of layers of sand, shell deposits, and clay.

It was 128 million years later when the oceans had receded that the Neuse River came along and started following a fault line we now call the fall line, where the rivers rambling from the Piedmont begin flowing more slowly and smoothly to the Atlantic Ocean.

I am most struck by how different this high riverbank is from all of the rest of the river, by how wonderful it is for photography vantage points, and how much gratitude we owe to Lionel Weil of Goldsboro, who spearheaded the campaign in the 1940's for the state of North Carolina to acquire this site as a state park. Weil actually bought several hundred acres around the Cliffs to donate to the state for this project.

This park is a living classroom for the river. Nature trails located throughout the park lead visitors to streambeds that flow into the Neuse. Looking at tributaries up close, actually wading in them, one has a far better chance of learning how important it is to protect what flows into the river in order to protect the river.

For the paddler making his way downriver from Falls Dam to Pamlico Sound, the Cliffs are right at the halfway mark, and as Marshall Ellis noted, both downwind and upwind of some of the best pit-cooked barbecue in the world.

Either before or after a meal of barbecue, slaw, hush puppies and sweet iced tea, a visit to this park is not a tourist stop.

A visit to this park is an opportunity to connect with a part of North Carolina's natural history.

Sailing

Oriental calls itself the Sailing Capital of North Carolina. There are more sailboats berthed at Oriental than there are permanent residents in this little fishing village by the river.

To understand anything about sailing, it helps to understand the people who sail. People who sail, and people who ride horses chasing little foxes through the woods, were most likely born under the same astrological sign.

I once knew quite a few people involved in foxhunting. Foxhunters demand a certain language style not common to us common folk.

For example, a foxhound is not a dog, it's a hound. If it looks like a dog and howls like a dog, I'm probably going to call it a dog.

Sailboat people borrowed their personalities from foxhunters because they adhere to a language of their own making, also.

For example, a rope on board a sailboat is not a rope, it's a line. It's rope when purchased at a marine supply store and rope when it is carried down to the dock, but when it is transferred onboard, it becomes a line.

Could have fooled me.

Let's do recognize that people who sail appreciate being on the water in a very special way, even though for the most part they have ignored the Industrial Revolution and prefer to depend on wind in sails instead of combustion in an engine.

Sailing, like negotiating whitewater in a canoe, is both an adventure and a challenge. It has poetically been called flying on water with the sails as the wings. It requires one to become the next of kin to water, to weather patterns over water, and to shoals under the water.

There are those for whom sailing is a spiritual happening, not necessarily a way to travel from port to port.

When my grandfather sailed from Oriental to New Bern in the late nineteenth century, he did so to get from Point A to Point B. Sailing was the practical means of travel from farm to market.

He told me of sailing home at night in cold winter winds. He said that when they saw a house on shore with a little light from a kerosene lantern seeping through windows, the vision of a family there all warm and cozy around the supper table made them feel a little warmer, knowing that they were on the way home to a table of hot food at the head of Smith Creek.

Even though my grandfather's sailing was for a practical means of transportation, his stories of sailing were rich in feeling. By not just listening to what he said, but also how he said it, I knew sailing was a spiritual experience for him.

So it is with sailors who will spend untold fortunes and endless hours maintaining a vessel strictly for the joy of hearing only wind above the waves propel the boat forward.

I retraced my grandfather's route on a sailboat with Richard deCharms and Marny Muir. I tried to visualize the river of one hundred years ago.

How much of the river now is the same? How much is different?

Snow

Immigrants to North Carolina from northern climes have difficulty in comprehending the impact of a forecast for snow on this region. At the mention of snow flurries by a weatherman, local grocery shelves are soon emptied of all the milk and bread.

In Eastern North Carolina, snow is not so much a weather event as it is a social happening. So it is for people who live along the Neuse River, especially those living by the more temperate lower river.

Here, seeing snow is about as rare as spotting a bald eagle preying over a catfish on a sandbar. Snow for those living downriver is almost a Blue Moon experience.

Just as whitewater on the river evokes danger, thrills, and a somewhat tranquil satisfaction, snow can blend hardship with quiet beauty and childlike excitement.

Because days on the river without snow so vastly outnumber days with snow, snow along this river calls for a holiday—time for everyone to become a photographer to capture the melting beauty, if not on film, at least in a memory bank.

Most people tend to think of the edge of the river as the riverbank or river shore. At so many places where the Neuse River meets terra firma, riverbanks are more like walls, especially from canoe vantage.

It is clearly obvious that some of these banks show what appears to be the effects of erosion. On the other hand, a leading geologist has tried desperately to explain to those who want to build along shorelines that sand doesn't erode. Sand adjacent to water's edge simply moves from place to place, when and where the water wants it to.

The walls along the Neuse vary from the ninety foot cliffs of sand, clay, and shell deposits in Wayne County to lines of cypress trees in Craven County, from clay banks in Johnston County, to the sandy ridges in Pamlico County.

Upon close inspection, one discovers that the walls are also tributaries. Steep banks of clay and sand are often like sieves draining the nearby groundwater into the river.

More reason to understand that what enters the land along the river also enters the river.

Tributaries

It is said that it takes a whole village to raise a child. So it can be said that it takes an entire river basin of tributaries to create a river.

Creeks, brooks, streams, and ditches all form the maze of pipelines that drain from the surrounding area into the Neuse.

I am not a hydrologist.

I know little about water flow or the geological make-up of rivers. But it doesn't take a rocket scientist to understand that the health of the tributaries determines the health of the river. What flows from the land surrounding the tributaries into the tributaries, naturally flows into the Neuse.

While chemical run-off is an obvious concern, the build-up of sandbars where creeks and ditches flow into the river is a telltale sign that sedimentation has a significant impact on the life of the river. Sedimentation is the consequence of too much development too close to the streams.

Past records indicate that large vessels plied the Neuse as far inland as Smithfield. It was really in recent times as far as river history goes, that the Confederate gunship, Ram Neuse, patrolled well beyond Kinston. Now, sedimentation has made it impossible for such vessels to navigate upriver. In the area where the Ram Neuse was found, a canoe can now run aground on sandbars in dry weather.

Like bridges, many such tributaries have names that reflect local history or folklore. Taylor Creek obviously honors someone named Taylor. Moccasin Creek needs no explanation. Kidney Creek, tucked away in a wilderness of cypress trees between New Bern and Kinston, allegedly resembles the shape of a kidney.

While it would be easy to use words like "swampy" or "murky" to describe these tributaries, I do not want to appear as negative in describing any part of the natural wonder of the Neuse. Where most creeks enter the river, one reacts to the visual scene immediately, wanting to capture on film the contrast between the shadows and streaks of sunlight filtering through the trees along the narrow streams.

Protecting tributaries is paramount to preserving more of the awesome beauty of the Neuse River.

The mention of whitewater evokes an anticipated thrill, as well as potential danger.

Water streaming rapidly over a rapid usually foams until the water is bubbly white. To paddle people in canoes or kayaks, whitewater is to them what the Tour de France is to Lance Armstrong. There is a double thrill: the experience itself, and then the joy of survival.

Beyond the thrills and danger involved in traversing through whitewater, there is the internal satisfaction of watching and listening to this phenomena. The sound of rushing water, just as rain pitter-pattering on a tin roof, provides a soothing for the soul.

Gunnison Rapids near Poole Road in Raleigh is officially classed as a Class II Rapids. On a scale of one-to-five, that degree of difficulty in negotiating the narrow channels between the big boulders indicates that novices should not be complacent.

Dave Mauney and I were not exactly complacent when our canoe became wedged between two rocks, perpendicular to the current.

It was funny when it was over, but only after we were back parallel with the current.

It is wrong to conclude that white-water is limited to where the river flows over and around the boulders in the rock gardens of the upper river. Whitewater occurs frequently in of the lower river. There, it appears as white caps, indicating at least a twelve-knot wind.

Just as with whitewater of the upper river, whitewater on the lower river is a thrill for those skipping across the waves on small sailboats. It remains a thrill until Small Craft Advisories become Small Craft Warnings, at which time the thrill transforms itself into danger.

And then there are times when the whitewater of the Neuse River has crashed against the front door of my house. Were it not for the danger and threat to life and property, there would be a thrill in watching the power of wind and water combined in that whitewater.

The rapid flow of whitewater will most assuredly bring on a rapid flow of adrenalin.

In St. Louis, the giant arch signals a gateway to the western half of this great land of America. All along the Neuse, arches formed by overhanging trees are gateways to ever-changing scenes of visual emotion.

The beauty of the trees that line the banks of the Neuse, and their importance to the life of the river and its wild habitat, are entities that must be protected and cherished for all ages.

In the last few years of the 20th century, hurricanes reduced many of these arches to barricades. While some arches leave little or no room for even a canoe to pass under, others have taken a place alongside the rocks and boulders to create a temporary whitewater scenario.

Trying to take a shortcut around a log jam in the stretch of river east of Richardson Bridge in Johnston County, Dave Mauney and I were first stuck on one log, freed ourselves to find the canoe parallel to that log and perpendicular to the rapid current, but parallel to another log just inches away. Sandwiched between two logs like a hot dog in a bun, we novices learned quickly how to remain calm.

I can testify that paddling a canoe is far less strenuous than cutting a path through a recently fallen oak for a jon boat and our accompanying equipment. I wonder who will find that sawblade we left pinched in a half sawn branch of that tree.

For the photographer, trees serve as a constant source of imagery. I found myself searching for the sun to highlight the willowy branches that draped over sandbar after sandbar. That contrast of light among leaves was highlighted by the contrast offered by so many contrasting varieties of trees.

Pine forests are common among the oaks of the middle river. As one travels downriver, cypress trees create shadows and shapes with their knees that stimulate the imagination to think of wild tales told by Southern writers like James Dickey or William Faulkner.

Add the clinging Spanish moss swinging overhead, and the feeling that one is a character in a mystery novel taking place in deep swamps makes imagination seem real.

Further downriver, trees that have fallen victim to storms become relics of driftwood that once were a source of fuel for men of earlier times, but are enjoyed in contemporary times for having intriguing ornamental shapes.

Now, more than ever, the forests along the banks of the Neuse are critically important as a buffer between the river and commercial and industrial development. The river was created without the presence of man. Man should do all he can to let the river and its trees have as little interference as possible from man.

Trees serve the river in ways other than for canoe adventures or as decoration. Trees are homesteads for wildlife.

If I had the gift of Joyce Kilmer, I could write volumes of poetry about the mystifying presence of trees that are all in one river.

Fog

I was first introduced to fog in poetry by a teacher sharing Carl Sandburg's version of fog creeping in on little cat's feet.

Bob Simpson, noted chronicler of life along North Carolina's coast, described fog as smoke over the water. When the air above the water has a much different temperature than the water, Simpson would say that the water smokes.

It doesn't matter whether one chooses to use the scientific, or the poetic, description of fog. The visual impact is spellbinding either way.

Seeing fog over the Neuse River, especially in the narrow reaches of the upriver, one becomes a player in the moving scenery. Smoke over the water upriver is another drama playing in an ethereal act of nature.

Fog is a dynamic feature of the lower river also, but more as a hazard to navigation. Just as with whitewater, that which adds drama can also add danger.

To Honor and Remember

Towers of the Neuse, cypress trees line the banks of this magical watershed much of the way from Raleigh to New Bern. Anchored on the river's edge with towering roots, cypress knees, and upper limbs adorned with Spanish moss, these towers paint a timeless landscape. Wavering reflections on the water's surface shimmer with the wind while the trees themselves are rooted In this coastal heritage.

For New Yorkers, the twin towers of The World Trade Center painted a landscape that was taken for granted to be as eternal as the majesty of the cypress towers of the Neuse River.

On September 11, 2001, I traveled with Richard deCharms and Marny Muir to Kinston and Goldsboro to view sites along The Neuse River for this photo-essay project.

Not fully aware of what was happening, we journeyed on to the Cliffs of The Neuse State Park, our ears glued to the car radio. Both of us becoming physically ill at the news, watching the peaceful countryside of North Carolina, picturing the havoc in New York, Washington and Pennsylvania, we hastened back to Pamlico County where the Neuse empties Into the Pamlico Sound.

In December of 2001, Dan Rather of CBS News interviewed six international photographers who were in New York on September 11. They all shared their emotions and photographs.

When asked about their thoughts of the future in light of this tragedy, one photographer replied that one must be like water. He observed that when water met a rock, it kept on going.

The Neuse River has met many adversaries, some natural, some man-made ....but it has kept on going.

To honor the memory of innocent civilians and courageous fire, police and rescue personnel lost on September 11, we must be like water. We must be like the Neuse River.

We must keep on going.

"The river connects people."

That's what my wife Emmy said after I returned from an early morning jaunt in the skiff following dolphins with a camera.

I told her about seeing two men in a small well-boat fishing crab pots. I stopped to speak to them and one of them said, "I know you. I'm Johnny Baldree."

Johnny Baldree was my older brother's high school friend. I had met Johnny Baldree, but not enough times and not recently enough to recognize him.

My brother grew up fishing the Neuse River and Pamlico County creeks that are part of the river's system of tributaries. In 1978, he visited Johnny Baldree, said to him, "Let's go fishing one more time."

They did.

Just a few days later, my brother took his life. He went back to this river, surely to connect with it one more time.

David Mauney's father fished this river every chance that he could. He grew up near its banks in Clayton. He retired to be near it in New Bern. When he died, he was returned to the river off Flanner's Beach.

I sat with Dave early one morning in the skiff at about the same place off Flanner's Beach where his father had been returned to the river.

Dave was re-living the connection his father had with the Neuse River.

Susan Sensenig from New Bern also has a permanent connection with the river. In early March of 2002, she and Chris Thomas discussed their plans for marriage, children and even what arrangements were desired when life for either of them on this earth should end.

She and Chris, when not working, were most likely to be found on the Neuse River. Chris had his private "honey holes," spots near the confluence of the Trent and Neuse Rivers where he had been quite successful catching rock fish.

In mid-March of 2002, Chris was the victim of a senseless murder by the hand of a stranger stealing his truck at his workplace.

After a funeral service at Union Point Park in New Bern, adjacent to one of the favorite "honey holes," Susan boarded a boat and returned him to the Neuse River for his final and eternal visit.

Many have been baptized in the Neuse River. Baptism is considered by some to be a form of birth.

Many have been married on the shores of the Neuse.

Many will be within the Neuse River for time everlasting.

So many people are connected to the river, and connected by the river, in so many ways.

*"So when you turn to look for me,
On the river is where I'll be...*

*'Remember me like this,' I ask,
And my memories will always last."*

FROM A TRIBUTE TO JAMES CHRISTOPHER THOMAS
BY CARL WYNN WHEELIS

...so the Neuse will flow pure and clear once more...

Dream of a Neuse safe for swimming children—a Neuse filled with plump, vigorous fish thriving in a healthy habitat—a Neuse whose water complements the beauty of its basin. For over twenty years, we have been working to restore your river to its ancient clarity, to cure its ills and keep them cured so the Neuse will flow pure and clear once more.

The Neuse River Foundation, its members and supporters, and its army of volunteers are on the job. Our Riverkeeper® is out there plying the wake of pioneer Rick Dove who accomplished so much. Tough boots to fill. Our new Upper Neuse Riverkeeper® is there also, working to stop pollution at it source before it blooms into a 200-mile toxic plume. Our volunteer Creekkeepers, Streamkeepers and Lakekeepers are spending precious hours patrolling the tributaries and testing the water. Our volunteer pilots are in the air, watching for signs of a river in trouble.

We have to keep at it all the time because entropy and apathy counter our efforts. So does ignorance. That is why we visit schools, teaching kids about their river and enlisting their help in our award-winning Little Riverwatchers program. And it is why we work with community leaders, civic groups, developers, and citizens, sharing our vision of what the Neuse can mean to them, and showing them what has to be done. And it is why we sponsor the yearly Neuse River Day for a special time of fun and education on the water.

Sometimes we have to do what no one else will because it is not pleasant or easy. We go to court to enforce clean water laws and to urge the enforcers to do what they must. We have to prove our case with facts and good science, and we have to know the law.

The Neuse River Foundation has over twenty-seven hundred loyal members committed to saving their river.

You have seen the beauty of the Neuse in this book and you have read its story. Now it is time to join us in restoring its waters. Please become a member by sending us the enclosed card, calling us at 252-637-7972, or joining on line at www.neuseriver.org.

NEUSE RIVER FOUNDATION, INC.
P. O. Box 15451
New Bern NC 28561
252-637-7972
252-514-0051 (fax)
info@neuseriver.org
www.neuseriver.org

Lower Neuse Riverkeeper®
220 South Front Street
New Bern, NC 28560
252-637-1970

Upper Neuse Riverkeeper®
112 South Blount Street
Raleigh NC 27601
919-856-1180

The Neuse River Foundation

THIS PUBLICATION WAS MADE POSSIBLE BY THE GENEROSITY OF THE FOLLOWING:

Jim & Barbara Goodmon
THE TRIANGLE COMMUNITY FUND
RALEIGH, NC

Mary Semans
THE MARY DUKE BIDDLE FOUNDATION
DURHAM, NC

Thomas & Wynn Kenworthy
ORIENTAL, NC

Structural Integrity Associates
ORIENTAL, NC

Dr. & Mrs. C. Vernon Rose
BAYBORO, NC

Richard deCharms & Marny Muir
ORIENTAL, NC

The Pamlico County Arts Council
BAYBORO, NC

Framer's Chop Service
ASHEVILLE, NC

Beth & Larry La Brie
PINE KNOLL SHORES, NC

Mr. & Mrs. AC Snow
RALEIGH, NC

Reverend Bob Inskeep
RALEIGH, NC

Earl Evens
ORIENTAL, NC

J. Keith Crisco
ASHEBORO, NC

Mae W. Bell
ROCKY MOUNT, NC

Ned Delamar, Sr.
ORIENTAL, NC

John S. & Patsy B. Carty
NASHVILLE, NC

Joe & Amy Wilson
NASHVILLE, NC

Don & Esther Williams
MERRITT, NC

Inland Waterway Treasure Company
ORIENTAL, NC

Judge Jim Ragan
ORIENTAL, NC

Radford & Jane Reel
NEW BERN, NC

Michael Projanski
NEW YORK, NY

Joyner's Supermarket
NASHVILLE, NC

Nora H. Kennel
KENNELS BEACH, NC

Mary Valentine McIntyre
NASHVILLE, NC

Katherine W. Scott
WILSON, NC

Dr. E. L. Elwood
RALEIGH, NC

Sail/Loft Realty
ORIENTAL, NC

Howard Andrews
ROCKY MOUNT, NC